Contents

Keep fit for footy

Injury is part of sport, it's true. But you can keep injuries to a minimum if you stick to these easy-to-follow rules:

Rule 1: Encase your body in cotton wool and run away crying if an opponent comes near you.

*Sorry, bit of a mix up. The **real** Rule 1 is ...*

Rule 1: Make sure you warm up before you play.

The warm-up depends on the sport. For footy, you need leg work such as light jogging, but tennis players will need to include arm work too. If you're a budding chess star, don't worry about the legs and arms, just blow hard on your fingers! For swimming, your warm-up can take place in the pool, as long as it doesn't include running or diving.

Stretches will help to ensure your joints are loose. Make sure you hold each stretch for 10 or 20 seconds and don't bounce up and down.

Rule 2: Take time to cool down after you play.

The cool-down activity gets the body back to its normal resting state at the correct rate, so you don't stiffen up too badly. Again, light jogging and stretches should do the trick.

Some kids pooh pooh this and say it has no use, but pro players from Liverpool to Newport County warm up and cool down before and after each game, so don't be a fool and don't make excuses – just do it!

Rule 3: Get the right kit.

For football, rugby or hockey:

⚽ Protect your feet with boots, not trainers, and make sure they fit snugly – not too tight or too loose. Make sure the studs in your boots are properly screwed in.

⚽ Wear shin pads to protect your legs from any nasty tackles.

For netball or tennis:

⚽ Wear a good pair of trainers to support your feet and your joints when you sprint and jump.

What injuries might I get?

An injury can happen if you play too much, or when you're tired. Remember, you need rest, or an injury can happen suddenly in a match. An acute injury (despite the name, it's not cute!) will often be a muscle strain or a sprained joint. These are common injuries in football because:

⚽ You do a lot of twisting and turning.

⚽ You often have to stop suddenly, then start running at full speed again very quickly.

⚽ Sprinting and tackling involve big, hard stretches. This is tough on the muscles in the back of the leg.

⚽ There's a lot of jumping and landing. Landing on hard ground puts strain on the knees. Landing on the side of the foot can result in a sprained ankle.

If you have this sort of injury, your ankle or knee will swell up and you'll be in a lot of pain. The best treatment is RICE. No, not fried or boiled, just RICE! It stands for:

R Rest

Stop running right away. Take it easy for a few days.

I Ice

Put some ice on it as soon as you can – this helps to bring the swelling down and stops you feeling the pain as much. Get a proper ice pack or just a bag of frozen peas from the freezer (wrap it up in a towel first, or it can stick to your skin and damage it). Leave it on for about 15 mins, then take it off for 20 mins. Repeat this, then serve the peas with fish and chips and ketchup (only kidding!).

C Compression

Put a bandage on to keep the swelling down, but make sure it's not too tight.

E Elevation

This means putting your leg up so that not as much blood flows to the injured part. Try mooching on the sofa with your leg up on pillows.

You **will** get an injury at some stage. Don't let it put you off. Take care, but keep on playing!

New school blues

Mr Booth: Ah, good morning, Mrs Gooch. I'm Mr Booth, the Headteacher. This must be Andrew. Good morning to you too, young man.

(No reply)

Mrs Gooch: Say hello to the Headteacher, Andrew.

Andrew: *(Mumbling)* 'Ello.

Mr Booth: Hmm. He doesn't exactly seem over the moon to be here.

Mrs Gooch: I'm afraid he's in a bit of a mood. You see, he really liked his old school. Didn't want to move away, did you, Son?

Andrew: No.

Mr Booth: Oh well, I expect he'll soon get used to it. Come on – I'll show you around. Would you like that, Andrew?

Andrew: *(Mumbling under his breath)* No.

Mr Booth: Sorry, what was that?

Mrs Gooch: *(Digging Andrew in the ribs)* He said he'd love it, Mr Booth.

Mr Booth: So, this is the Year 7 corridor, and this is our new Technology room.

(Mr Booth pushes open the door, and a wave of noise hits them.)

Mrs Gooch: They seem a little ... lively.

Mr Booth: Oh, don't worry, Mrs Gooch. Here at Homelands School, we like children to have fun and enjoy themselves.

Mrs Gooch: Yes, but are you sure that's safe? In a Technology room, I mean?

Mr Booth: Of course it ... *(shouts suddenly)* Jessica! Put that down! Remember the school rules: it's rude to glue a teacher's jacket to the chair.

Jack, please don't rock back on your stool, or you'll end up ... oh dear, too late. Could someone escort Jack to the school nurse, please? And get the floor cleaned up.

Andrew: Cool! I think I'm going to like it here after all.

Mrs Gooch: Perhaps we should move on, Mr Booth.

Mr Booth: Yes, of course. As it's nearly lunch time, let's pay a visit to the canteen.

Mrs Gooch: (*Shivering*) Brr, it's a bit chilly in here, Mr Booth. And why are the children all wearing coats?

Andrew: (*Pointing up*) There's a great big hole in the roof, that's why.

Mr Booth: Ah, you spotted the hole. Yes, I'm afraid we had a slight accident last Friday. Cook forgot to take the roast chicken out and the stove exploded. Never mind, as long as it's not raining, things are fine.

(*Dark spots begin to appear on the floor*)

Andrew: (*Holding hand out*) I thought I felt a raindrop.

Mr Booth: Nonsense, I'm sure that's just, er, condensation or something.

Mrs Gooch: The food looks a bit ... odd, Mr Booth. What are they eating?

Mr Booth: Hmm, looks like stewed prunes on toast.

Andrew: Yuk!

Mr Booth: Yes, well it's difficult to stick to the menu when you haven't got a cooker.

Andrew: Let's get out of here, Mum, before I throw up!

Mr Booth: Here we are at the swimming pool. We pride ourselves on being the only school in Blackpool with a pool. This will be your new class, Andrew – 7G. They're having a swimming lesson with Mr Askew, our PE teacher.

(Lots of moans, groans and spluttering can be heard as the teacher barks instructions.)

Mrs Gooch: Hmm. He seems a bit strict.

Mr Booth: Oh, we like our children to be fit and strong, Mrs Gooch. Mr Askew works them hard, but if they look as if they're about to choke, we fish them out with a big pole, and we've only had to phone for an ambulance twice this week.

Mrs Gooch: I didn't think children were supposed to run around in a swimming pool.

Mr Booth: You're quite right. *(Shouts)* Be careful Lewis, or you'll bump into some—

(Splash!)

Mr Booth: Oh dear. Did Andrew bring a spare set of clothes, Mrs Gooch?

The flight of Freddy Fish

I've had that puffer fish as a personal trainer. I'm super fit. Fifty laps of the tank each day.

Oh, now I understand. I thought you were just having one of your odd months.

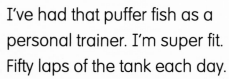

FASTER!

Not at all. I'm fitter than that Bockham bloke on the telly. Fins of steel!

OK, just say you *can* get out of the tank, what then? You going to swim across the carpet, open the back door and leg it? Sorry, I mean fin it?

It won't work.

Yes it will. You're just bitter because I've got such a cracker of a plan and you admire it.

That's exactly what I plan to do.

OK, OK, keep your scales on. What about Nabber, that ginger monster? Cats love fish.

He'll catch you, bother you, batter you ... then have your fishy fingers for dinner.

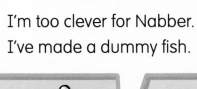

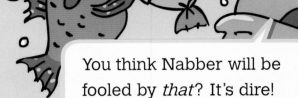

14

The dog ate my homework!

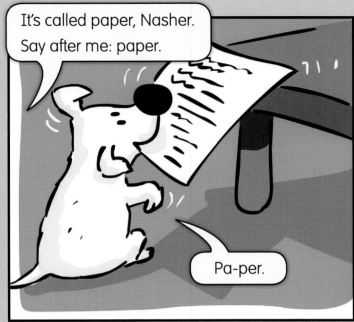

Monday, 21st October, 9.07 a.m.

Later …

Life on a cattle ranch

Do you ever watch cowboy films? The cowboys of the 1800s always seemed to be having battles with American Indians, or outlaws. But cowboys still exist today, working on cattle ranches in North and South America and Australia. Their lives are very different.

Matthew is 13, and he lives on a cattle ranch in North America. Let him tell you about his unusual life.

My dad has about two hundred cattle, and it's his job to raise them and sell them for beef. I help him and his staff whenever I'm available – I do have to go to school as well! Most ranch work is done on horseback, but nowadays we use trucks, too. You have to be fit and strong to work on a ranch – it's very hard work.

I started riding when I was little – as soon as I could sit on a saddle! My horse is chestnut-brown, and his name is Firebrand. He comes when I whistle, and then I put on his tasselled blanket, his saddle and his bridle. I always wear my cowboy boots when I ride Firebrand, because they protect my feet and ankles. It's a ranch hand's job to brush the horse and untangle his mane and tail.

Spring is a busy time on the ranch, because that's the time when the calves are born. There are usually about a hundred, and I help to look after them.

Our other busy time is when we do the round-up, which happens twice a year. It means at least a day in the saddle, and we get very sore. We ride out to the places where the cattle are grazing, and bring the herd back to the ranch. At lunch time, we sit on the ground and eat a picnic – mostly it's hot chilli made from chunks of beef. Back at the ranch, we sort and count the cattle, and take out the ones that are going to be sold. We also brand the new calves – mark them with a hot branding iron. Every ranch has its own special mark.

To take part in the round-up, you must be able to rope cattle. These days our ropes are made of nylon, a very strong material. The coiled rope is kept on the raised pommel (front) of the saddle. Sometimes we do team roping – two men work together, one on each side of a single running cow or bull. One man has to throw a rope round the front of the cow, and the other throws a rope round the back. That's pretty hard – and we have to do it when we are hurtling along on the back of a galloping horse! And yes, we do need to practise!

At other times of the year, there is always plenty to do – repairing equipment, cleaning saddles and bridles and doing odd jobs. In the winter, the weather can be terrible, with lots of ice and snow, but we still have to work outside on the ranch.

I really like going to the local rodeo. Lots of people go to this cowboy festival, to watch daredevils competing to stay on the back of a bucking horse (bucking bronco). In some trials, at the top level, they have to do it bareback (without a saddle). For all but the top riders, this is practically impossible.

Do I like living and working on a ranch? Yes, it's cool. I love working with animals, and if possible, I want to train to be a vet. But it's a hard job. Could *you* do it?

Watch that turtle hurtle!

Animal races have always been popular spectator events. However, many people think that animal racing is a cruel sport and should be banned. Read this text and see what you think.

Horse races take place every day, all around the world. You may have seen greyhound races too, where six dogs chase round a track after an electrical hare. But horses and greyhounds are expensive and, depending on where you live, they might not be easily available. So different creatures need to be found – some more unusual than others!

Let's start with the biggest and work our way down ...

On your marks ...

An **elephant** racing festival takes place every year in the jungles of Vietnam. Up to ten huge beasts battle it out over a short course. Each elephant is ridden by two men – one in front who urges it to go faster, and one behind who tries to steer it in a straight line.

Camel racing is an extremely popular sport in the Middle East. Similar to horse racing, the camels are saddled and ridden by small jockeys around an oval-shaped track. Some camels can gallop around the course at speeds of up to 40mph!

In parts of Africa, camels are substituted with **ostriches**. They are equally speedy, but can be rather temperamental and difficult to handle. This demands great skill from their riders.

Cattle and **buffalo** races are a common sight in the muddy fields of south Asia. Two cows are harnessed together, with the jockey balanced on a narrow sled between them. The jockey has to tackle a nearly impossible double task – holding on to both animals while trying to make sure they run at the same speed through the puddles.

If you find yourself wandering through the little English village of Bonsall on the first Saturday in August, you will be able to settle down to witness the World **Hen** Racing Championships! The rival hens race over a 10m track, helping to raise money for local charities.

Get set ...

At some fairs and festivals in the USA, **turtles** are placed in the centre of a large circle. When the whistle goes, the winner of the gold medal is the turtle which hurtles (well, OK, plods actually) out of the circle before any of the others.

Did you know?

A similar (but slightly more disgusting) race takes place each year on Australia's National Day. Instead of turtles hurtling out of the circle, it's ... cockroaches. Yuk! Better not sit in the front row!

Perhaps the speediest racers of all are **pigeons** (no jockeys needed!). Specially trained to find their way home from great distances, these feathery marvels are driven up to a thousand miles away before being released on race day. Homing pigeons can fly at over 60mph. The trouble is, some birds of prey can fly even faster, so sadly not all pigeons complete the race.

A growing sport in the UK in the 21st century is, believe it or not, hamster racing! The cuddly rodents race their transparent hamster balls along a track 2–9 m long. Some owners customise their hamster balls to look like racing cars. Have they totally lost their marbles?

Go!!!

And finally, our smallest racers: slippery, slimy **snails**. Their shells are painted so they're easy to spot, and these slowcoaches can actually cover the 35cm course in a dazzling time of ... not much over 3 minutes. Blink and you definitely won't miss this one!

Odd achievements

Do any of your mates do strange things? They won't seem so strange when you have read about these odd achievements! And yes, it's all true!

Lee Redmond from the USA hasn't cut her nails since 1979! How odd is that? These magnificent nails reached 865cm long! How does she eat, or dress – or even scratch her nose?

A Russian woman and her husband had 69 children! These proud parents had 16 pairs of twins, 7 sets of triplets and 4 sets of quads. What are the chances of that?

In 2003, American Ron Hunt had an awful experience. He fell off a ladder – and on to a drill bit that was 46cm long. It went straight through his skull – but it missed his brain. With good medical treatment, lucky Ron survived to tell the tale!

New Zealander Robert Thomson travelled a distance of 12,159km to make his record-breaking skateboard ride. He went all the way from Switzerland to China, and it took him 15 months!

When American Claudia Mitchell had a motorbike accident in 2006, she lost an arm. Doctors fitted her with a replacement – the world's first bionic arm! If she wants to move her arm, her brain sends a message to it.

A pro referee at almost 9 years old – cool! Instant fame for Samuel Keplinger, the ref in a football match in Germany in 2008.

And now for the bloke who eats metal! There is evidence that Frenchman Michel Lotito has eaten: 15 supermarket trolleys, 18 bikes, 7 TV sets, 2 beds, a pair of skis, a light aircraft and a computer.

The tallest man ever is Robert Wadlow, from the USA. The measurement from head to toe of this giant person was 2.72m. Quite a distance!

Benedikt Weber, a German reporter, drank a bottle of ketchup through a straw in a record-breaking 32.37 seconds. What a performance!

Walking on hot coals is not a pleasant thing to do, to say the least. But to the astonishment of his audience, Brit Scott Bell walked across burning embers for a distance of 100m in China in 2006.

How's this for a hat? It beats a baseball cap any day! In 1999, John Evans (another Brit) balanced a car on his head, to the amazement of the crowd. It was a red Mini, and John kept it on his head for 33 seconds. His extra-thick neck allowed him to do it. Since then, no opponent has matched John's achievement.

Why don't you try for a world record?

You could have a go at making the biggest-ever ball of sticky tape (the current record-holder weighs 907.18kg). Or try for this important record – throwing more than 24 custard pies in a minute? Or push an orange with your nose – can you beat a distance of 1.6km in 22 minutes and 41 seconds?

The featured records have been supplied courtesy of Guinness Book of Records Limited.

Emergency – the A and E department

(An A and E department. A nurse stands behind the reception desk. A very elegant lady walks in with a large snake wrapped tightly around her neck.)

Nurse Florence: Good morning, madam. What seems to be the trouble?

Snake Lady: Are you kidding?

Nurse Florence: No, madam. Now what's the problem?

Snake Lady: Can't you see? I've got a snake wrapped round my neck!

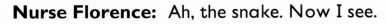

Nurse Florence: Ah, the snake. Now I see.

Snake Lady: *(Under her breath)* Brilliant! How very observant you are.

Nurse Florence: *(Talking while writing on form)* … Serpent … around … neck. Jolly good. Would you like to make an appointment? Dr Scales is free next Friday morning at … let me see … 10.20.

Snake Lady: Next Friday? This is urgent! It's choking me!

Nurse Florence: *(Writing)* … Urgent … choking. Very well, madam. Please take a seat and a consultant will be with you shortly.

Snake Lady: Incompetent fool!

Snake Lady: What's *he* doing down there?

Nurse Florence: He's a doctor.
He's very overworked.
He's just having
a quick nap.

Snake Lady: Can't you shift him?
He's an inconvenience
down there, blocking
the entrance.

Nurse Florence: No, madam.
He needs his sleep.

Doctor: Zzzzzz …

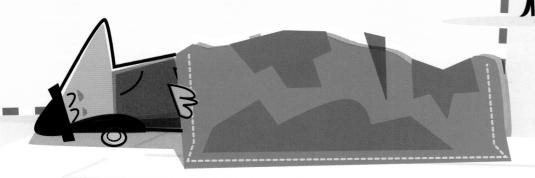

(Paramedics rush in with a man. His hands are heavily bandaged.)

Nurse Florence: Oh no, not you again.

Professor Chance: Sorry, I seem to have a talent for blowing myself up, don't I?

Nurse Florence: What was it this time?

Professor Chance: Oh, just an experiment to try to make petrol from instant coffee.

Nurse Florence: You're a constant pain – in and out of here every week. Let's have a look. Hmm, damage to the thumb looks permanent this time. I'm sorry, but you'll never play the violin again.

Professor Chance: That's OK. I couldn't play it before.

Snake Lady: *(Interrupting loudly)* Where's the consultant? I demand to see the consultant!

(The noise startles the snake, which starts hissing loudly.)

Nurse Florence: Now now, madam, don't be so impatient. And can you please silence your serpent? It's upsetting the other patients.

(Enter police officer with a teenager in a baseball cap.)

Policeman: Excuse me, miss. This lad's been bitten by my dog.

Nurse Florence: Ah, I see.

Policeman: He's a persistent truant. The boy, that is, not Rover. We spotted him on Regent Street. He legged it, we gave chase, and he ended up with a bottom full of teeth.

Nurse Florence: Hmm. Are you all right, boy? *(No answer)* Hello? Is there intelligent life under that cap?

Boy: This place is a dump. It stinks of disinfectant.

Policeman: Can we hurry up please, nurse? It's important that I take a statement.

Nurse Florence: Well, the treatment is a tetanus jab.

(To boy) You may experience a sharp sting and then some slight tingling.

Boy: Ouch!

34

Policeman: Right, come on then, lad. First the police station, then back to school.

Nurse Florence: Good riddance, I say. These truants are a right nuisance. I blame the parents. They're such a bad influence.

Snake Lady: Will somebody get me the consultant?!

Consultant: (*Walking in*) Hello, madam. Can I be of any assistance?

Snake Lady: I hope so. I'm waiting to see the consultant.

Consultant: That's me, madam. Now, what seems to be the trouble?

Snake Lady: I don't believe this! I've got a snake wrapped round my neck!

Consultant: Ah, the snake's the problem, is it? I thought it was just a fashion statement. Well, don't worry, we'll soon fix it. Nurse, hand me the anti-serpent ointment, please. Now, if we just rub this into your neck, the snake should slide off when we pull. Ready? One … two … three … pull!

(The snake shoots off the lady's neck and flies through the air. Patients look on in amazement.)

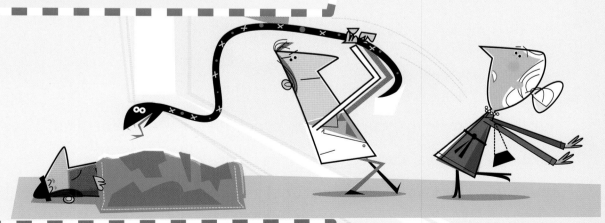

Doctor: (*Waking up in puzzlement*) Where am I? And what's this snake doing round my neck?

Creature features!

Horror movies – which one of us doesn't get pleasure from going to the pictures to be frightened out of our wits every now and again? Film directors understand human behaviour and know how to play about with the things that make us feel unsure and insecure.

But no fantasy film would be complete without the special effects (SFX) department's skills! They have to labour away to manufacture a creature that has convincing features – to create a creature or monster that matches the splendour of its creator's description! Very tricky. It is all too easy to make a monster that falls short of being, well, monster-like.

Not all horror pictures have specially made creatures. Top make-up artists can take a film star known for his or her glamour and turn them into a prematurely old, disfigured, terrifying creature that even their own granny would not recognise! The make-up artist has all sorts of stuff in their kit to transform a natural beauty into a very unnatural horror.

Think of the victim of an attack — the actor has to look injured, but make-up artists must make sure they are not harmed in real life. Imagine the pressure of "disfiguring" a multi-million dollar box office star!

Before make-up

After make-up

In their kit-bag, you can be sure a make-up artist will have a substance called liquid latex. It is perfect for creating the texture of damaged skin or changing the structure or shape of a face. Special soft, skin-coloured wax is used for changing the contours of faces by adding bumps, lumps and scars.

A pot called a "bruise wheel" has six colours (shades of blue, green and purple) to create the effect of bruising. The pallor (pale look) of a badly injured victim can be manufactured by using a pot called a "death wheel"! Sounds grim (and painful!) but it just has coloured make-up in very pale shades to give that "I am about to die ..." look.

And teeth? Yes, you could have a lot of fun turning gleaming celebrity teeth into rotting stumps with a bottle containing a mixture called black tooth enamel, which has a special applicator.

In fact, there is nothing that you can't buy to conjure up the most incredible special effects. They even manufacture artificial vomit!

I bet you'd love to have a go at special effect make-up, wouldn't you? Well you don't need lots of money to get hours of pleasure turning willing victims (er ... mates) into revolting creatures. A few bits and bobs from the kitchen or bathroom, plus a bit of skin-coloured make-up (beg from Mum) and you can create a gruesome torture victim, or just a good old monster!

To create the pale skin, or pallor, of an injured person, use a little talcum powder on top of skin-coloured make-up. A mixture of blue, green and purple eye shadow can really capture that bruised look.

To make brilliant warts, I favour crispy rice cereal! Anchor them to skin with a bit of sticky honey. They look very natural (and you can eat them afterwards).

For some realistic looking stitches (called sutures in medical procedures), use a thin eyebrow pencil to draw a long line on a cheek, then add short, vertical lines through the horizontal line.

For a gruesome-looking gash on an arm or leg, follow this procedure:

Make a mixture of some petroleum jelly, red food colouring or face paint and a bit of hot chocolate powder (for darker "blood"). Ensure it is well mixed. Rip a bit of tissue up and put on the spot where you want your gash to be.

Dab the jelly mixture on the tissue. Apply pressure to get the shape and texture of a nasty cut. Make sure the edges are jagged like a real gash. Add trickles of bright red face paint to contrast with the darker, dried "blood" inside the cut! Pure gore!

Happy horror days!

MONSTER

I was called a mutant,
a monster,
a creature of the dead.
Formed not like you,
by nature,
but made by man instead.

I am a crazy mixture,
of body parts
fused together and used again.
I was made by Dr Frankenstein.
You may have heard his name?

As he plotted each procedure,
excitement
in him
blazed.
His pallor showed his weariness
and his eyes showed he was crazed.

With a fever and such fervour,
he laboured
each
long
hour.
The young doctor stopped eating
and sleeping.
From his work he gained his power.

He sewed the parts together,
added details to my face.
He wired me up on a stormy night
in a dark and secret place.

A charge of electricity,
a blinding
flash
of light!
The sky lit up
as lightning struck.
My future began that night . . .

But the joy my creator felt,
to horror quickly turned.
He saw, not a man, but a monster.
His shame and terror burned.

I, the creature who stood before him,
was huge,
grotesque
and wild.
I knew that moment, wherever I went,
I'd be hated, feared, reviled.

The doctor ran away from me,
as others would run or hide.
They only saw a monster,
not my human heart inside.

What torture I felt in my loneliness,
my sorrowful,
nightmare
life.
I longed for human kindness
and the joy of a loving wife.

But none of these pleasures were ever mine.
No saviour
changed
my fate.
So I did become a monster,
full of pure rage, fear and hate.

Foolish Dr Frankenstein!

I was your labour of love;
treasured dream and path to fame.
I was your triumph and your failure.
For in me they were both the same ...

Keep fit for footy (ew ear)

Green words: *Say the sounds. Say the word.*

tru<u>e</u>   c<u>u</u>te   r<u>u</u>le   scr<u>ew</u>   f<u>ew</u>   n<u>ear</u>

Say the syllables. Say the word.

Liv|<u>er</u>|pool   ex|c<u>u</u>ses   a|c<u>u</u>te

Say the root word. Say the whole word.

m<u>oo</u> <u>ch</u> ➡ m<u>oo</u> <u>ch</u>ing

Red words: d<u>oe</u>sn't   any   <u>sh</u> <u>ould</u>   c<u>ome</u>s   <u>th</u> <u>ere</u>   s<u>ome</u>

Challenge words: w<u>ar</u>m   ens<u>ure</u>   t<u>ou</u> <u>gh</u>   compre<u>ss</u>ion   eleva<u>ti</u>on   w<u>ear</u>
cry<u>ing</u>   s<u>ure</u>   w<u>or</u>k   w<u>orr</u>y   mus<u>c</u>le

Vocabulary check: **compression** *to squeeze or press hard on something*
elevation *to lift up or raise something*
acute injury *an injury that has happened by one single accident*

New school blues (ew ear)

Green words: *Say the sounds. Say the word.*

n<u>ew</u>   r<u>u</u>les   r<u>u</u>de   gl<u>ue</u>   pr<u>u</u>nes   <u>year</u>   d<u>ear</u>

Say the syllables. Say the word.

An|dr<u>ew</u>   Bla<u>ck</u>|pool   As|k<u>ew</u>   L<u>ew</u>|is   n<u>ear</u>|ly   a<u>pp</u>|<u>ear</u>

Say the root word. Say the whole word.

<u>u</u>se ➡ <u>u</u>sed   st<u>ew</u> ➡ st<u>ew</u>ed

Red words: lo<u>ve</u>   d<u>oe</u>sn't   h<u>ere</u>   w<u>ould</u>   s<u>ome</u>one   <u>sh</u> <u>ould</u>   <u>th</u> <u>ough</u>t
gr<u>ea</u>t   c<u>ome</u>

Challenge words: w<u>orr</u>y   w<u>ear</u>ing   s<u>ure</u>   condensa<u>ti</u>on   <u>why</u>   <u>you</u> <u>ng</u>   mo<u>ve</u>
br<u>ea</u><u>th</u>   c<u>our</u> <u>se</u>   menu   h<u>ear</u>d   w<u>or</u>ks

Vocabulary check: **escort** *go somewhere with someone who is going to guide or protect you*
condensation *water which collects as droplets on a cold surface*

The flight of Freddy Fish (ire)

Green words: *Say the sounds. Say the word.*

tired   dire

Say the syllables. Say the word.

ad|mire   en|tire|ly   gin|ger   hatt|er   puff|er   fing|ers   bitt|er   crack|er
dress|er   both|er   shatt|er   re|mem|ber   clev|er   simpl|er   un|der|stand

Red words: thought   love   there   water   were   through

Challenge words: world   months   sure   wondered   work   nothing

Vocabulary check: **shatter** *smash or break*

The dog ate my homework! (ire)

Green words: *Say the sounds. Say the word.*

tired   wire   fire

Say the sylables. Say the word.

Oc|to|ber   Pe|ter   Park|er   Butch|er   ham|ster   mys|ter|y
mast|er   re|mem|ber   trou|sers   lat|er   train|ers   tas|ti|er   kill|er

Red words: mother   here   called   some   great   love   son

Challenge words: homework   earlier   ironed   half   hour   wearing   honest
they're   find   mystery   try   done   human   washing   ideal   course

Vocabulary check: **dresser** *a sideboard with shelves for displaying plates*   **peckish** *hungry*

Life on a cattle ranch (_il _al _ve)

Green words: *Say the syllables. Say the word.*

brid|le   catt|le   batt|les   sadd|le   untang|le   ank|les

pomm|el   sing|le   mat|e|ri|al   un|us|u|al   spe|cial   an|i|mal

lo|cal   terr|ib|le   im|poss|ib|le   a|vail|ab|le

Red words: comes   watch   oth er   people   could   some   love

---

Challenge words: Australia   always   also   front   busy   work   done

whistle   wear   cal ves   wea th er

Vocabulary check: grazing *cattle slowly eating the grass and plants around them*

bridle *harness that goes over the horse's head*

saddle *leather seat that straps on to a horse so we can ride it*

Watch that turtle hurtle! (_il _al _ve)

Green words: *Say the syllables. Say the word.*

riv|al   fin|all|y   hur|tle   el|ec|tri|cal   a|vail|a|ble   un|us|u|al

fes|ti|val   jun|gles   batt|le   Midd|le   catt|le   tack|le

im|poss|ib|le   doub|le   pudd|les   prin|ci|ple   mar|bles

Say the root word. Say the whole word.

sadd le → sadd led   equal → equ all y

Red words: wa tch   many   wh ere   th ey   some   oth ers   through   people
sh ould   small   great   th eir   any   balls

Challenge words: greyhound   creatures   cour se   fields   wandering   centre
pigeons   always   popular   world   double   sure   money   whistle   instead
trouble   prey   cover   minutes

Vocabulary check: spectator *a person who watches an event*   **substituted** *replaced with another*
temperamental *often has changes in mood*   **harnessed** *tied with straps*
sled *sledge*   **transparent** *see-through, clear*

Odd achievements (_ent _ence _ant _ance)

Green words: *Say the syllables. Say the word.*

gi|ant   curr|ent   ex|per|i|ence   plea|sant   au|di|ence

Say the root word. Say the whole word.

measure → measurement   achieve → achievement   astonish → astonishment

replace → replacement   evident → evidence   distant → distance

treat → treatment   perform → performance

Red words: walking   another   through   any   does   tallest   could

Challenge words: read   woman   parents   breaking   months   world   move
measurement   head   pleasant   another   John   minutes

Vocabulary check: bionic arm *a false arm controlled by a person's thoughts*
astonishment *amazement*

Emergency – the A and E department (_ent _ence _ant _ance)

Green words: *Say the syllables. Say the word.*

de|part|ment   in|com|pet|ent   in|con|ven|i|ence   per|man|ent   si|lence
tru|ant   ridd|ance   in|flu|ence

Say the root word. Say the whole word.
persist → persistance   disinfect → disinfectant   treat → treatment
assist → assistance

Red words: walks   other   come   they're   through   where   talking
would   couldn't   some   thought   should

Challenge words: trouble   loses   patients   answer   station   nuisance
breath   overworked   heavily   worry   ready

Vocabulary check: incompetent *not having the skills to do something properly*
inconvenience *cause trouble or difficulty*   **persistent** *continuing to try at something*
truant *a pupil who stays away from school without explanation*   **consultant** *a specialist doctor*

Creature features (_ture _ure _our _or)

Green words: *Say the sounds. Say the word.*

p<u>ure</u>   <u>s</u>ure

Say the syllables. Say the word.

<u>crea</u>|ture   su|t<u>ure</u>s   struct|<u>ure</u>   dis|fig|<u>ure</u>d   in|sec|<u>ure</u>   plea|<u>s</u>ure

pre|mat|<u>ure</u>ly   man|u|fac|ture   con|j<u>ure</u>   cap|ture   tex|ture   con|t<u>our</u>s

col|<u>our</u>s   la|b<u>our</u>   fa|v|<u>our</u>   pa|<u>ll</u> or   an|<u>ch</u> or   ho|<u>rr</u> or   be|ha|vi|<u>our</u>

Red words: <u>through</u>   d<u>oe</u>sn't   w<u>ou</u>ld   c<u>ou</u>ld   ca<u>ll</u>ed

---

Challenge words: br<u>ui</u> se   afterw<u>ar</u>ds   human   mon<u>ey</u>   b<u>uy</u>   <u>eye</u>   hon<u>ey</u>

mov<u>ie</u>s   b<u>eau</u>ty   no<u>th</u>ing   w<u>ar</u>ts   c<u>e</u>real   bl<u>oo</u>d

---

Vocabulary check: pallor *unhealthy looking, pale skin colour*

sutures *stitches in a wound*   **spectators** *an audience – people watching an event*

prematurely *too early – before the expected time*   **contours** *features*

Monster (_ture _ure _our _or)

Green words: *Say the sounds. Say the word.*

p<u>ure</u>

Say the syllables. Say the word.

<u>crea</u>|ture   na|ture   pro|ce|d<u>ure</u>   pa|<u>ll</u> or   ferv|<u>our</u>   doc|tor   fu|ture

cre|a|tor   tor|ture   plea|<u>s</u>ures   sav|i|<u>our</u>   f<u>ai</u>l|<u>ure</u>   mix|ture   ho|<u>rr</u> or

Say the root word. Say the whole word.

la<u>b</u><u>our</u> ➔ la<u>b</u><u>our</u>ed   tr<u>ea</u><u>s</u>ure ➔ tr<u>ea</u><u>s</u>ured

---

Red words: <u>oth</u> ers   <u>th</u> <u>ey</u>   w<u>e</u>re   ca<u>ll</u>ed   lo<u>ve</u>

Challenge words: Frankenst<u>ei</u>n   h<u>ear</u>d   <u>eye</u>s   <u>you</u>ng   <u>s</u>ewed   grotes<u>que</u>   human

h<u>ear</u>t   w<u>or</u>k   non<u>e</u>   h<u>our</u>

Vocabulary check: fused *joined together*   **pallor** *unhealthy looking, pale skin colour*

weariness *extreme tiredness*   **fervour** *dedication and passion*   **reviled** *criticised or insulted*

saviour *rescuer*